Pebble™ Plus

Mighty Machines

Dump Trucks

by Linda D. Williams

Consulting Editor: Gail Saunders-Smith, PhD
Consultant: Debra Hilmerson, Member
American Society of Safety Engineers
Des Plaines, Illinois

Capstone
press

Mankato, Minnesota

Pebble Plus is published by Capstone Press
151 Good Counsel Drive, P.O. Box 669, Mankato, Minnesota 56002
www.capstonepress.com

1 2 3 4 5 6 09 08 07 06 05 04

Library of Congress Cataloging-in-Publication Data
Williams, Linda D.
    Dump trucks / by Linda D. Williams.
    p. cm.—(Pebble plus: mighty machines)
    Includes bibliographical references and index.
    ISBN 0-7368-2596-7 (hardcover)
    1. Dump trucks—Juvenile literature. [1. Dump trucks.] I. Title. II. Series.
TL230.15.W553 2005
629.225—dc22   2003025766

Summary: Simple text and photographs present dump trucks and the work they do.

Editorial Credits
Martha E. H. Rustad, editor; Molly Nei, designer; Scott Thoms, photo researcher;
    Karen Hieb, product planning editor

Photo Credits
Bruce Coleman Inc./M. H. Black, 18–19
constructionphotography.com, 1, 6–7, 17
Corbis/Lester Lefkowitz, cover, 8–9; Roger Ressmeyer, 4–5; Paul Steel, 10–11; Royalty Free, 12–13;
    Tim Wright, 20–21
Index Stock Imagery/Tom Carroll, 14–15

Note to Parents and Teachers

The Mighty Machines series supports national standards related to science, technology, and society. This book describes and illustrates dump trucks. The images support early readers in understanding the text. The repetition of words and phrases helps early readers learn new words. This book also introduces early readers to subject-specific vocabulary words, which are defined in the Glossary section. Early readers may need assistance to read some words and to use the Table of Contents, Glossary, Read More, Internet Sites, and Index/Word List sections of the book.

Word Count: 119
Early-Intervention Level: 13

Table of Contents

Dump Trucks 4

Dump Truck Parts. 8

What Dump Trucks Do. . . . 14

Mighty Machines 20

Glossary. 22

Read More 23

Internet Sites 23

Index/Word List. 24

Dump Trucks

Dump trucks carry

and dump.

Loaders fill dump trucks
with sand and rocks.
Dump trucks carry
heavy loads.

Dump Truck Parts

Dump truck drivers sit in cabs. Drivers control dump trucks. Cabs keep drivers safe from falling rocks.

cab

Dump truck beds tip up.

Loads slide out into piles.

bed

Dump trucks have big tires.
Some dump trucks have
tires that are taller
than a person.

13

What Dump Trucks Do

Dump trucks carry lots of rocks and dirt. A dump truck could carry the weight of many elephants.

15

Dump trucks carry sand and gravel. They also carry broken concrete.

17

Dump trucks work in pit
mines and at building sites.
Dump trucks carry dirt
for roads and parks.

Mighty Machines

Dump trucks carry
and dump loads. Dump
trucks are mighty machines.

Glossary

bed—the back end of a dump truck; the bed tips up to dump loads.

building site—a place where something new is being made or constructed

cab—an area for a driver to sit in a large truck or machine, such as a dump truck

gravel—a mixture of sand, pebbles, and broken rocks

load—anything that must be lifted and carried by a person or machine

loader—a machine that lifts and carries loads

pit mine—a deep, open hole in the earth where minerals are found

Read More

Bridges, Sarah. *I Drive a Dump Truck.* Minneapolis: Picture Window Books, 2004.

Jango-Cohen, Judith. *Dump Trucks.* Pull Ahead Books. Minneapolis: Lerner, 2003.

Randolph, Joanne. *Dump Trucks.* Earth Movers. New York: PowerKids Press, 2002.

Internet Sites

FactHound offers a safe, fun way to find Internet sites related to this book. All of the sites on FactHound have been researched by our staff.

Here's how:

1. Visit *www.facthound.com*

2. Type in this special code **0736825967** for age-appropriate sites. Or enter a search word related to this book for a more general search.

3. Click on the **Fetch It** button.

FactHound will fetch the best sites for you!

Index/Word List

beds, 10

building sites, 18

cabs, 8

carry, 4, 6, 14, 16,
 18, 20

concrete, 16

control, 8

dirt, 14, 18

drivers, 8

gravel, 16

loaders, 6

loads, 6, 10, 20

machines, 20

mighty, 20

parks, 18

piles, 10

pit mines, 18

roads, 18

rocks, 6, 8, 14

safe, 8

sand, 6, 16

slide, 10

tip, 10

tires, 12

weight, 14

work, 18